STRANGE SHAPE

Cat Woodward

Strange Shape
Copyright © Cat Woodward, 2024

Cover design & typesetting: Natty Peterkin

ISBN 9781912665327

Cat Woodward has asserted her right under Section 77 of the Copyright, Designs and Patents Act 1988 to be identified as the author of this work.

All rights reserved. No part of this publication may be reproduced, stored in a retrieval system, or transmitted in any form or by any means, graphic, electronic, recorded, mechanical, or otherwise, without the prior written permission of the publisher or copyright holder.

This publication is sold subject to the condition that it shall not, by way of trade or otherwise, be lent, re-sold, hired out or otherwise circulated without the publisher's prior consent in any form of binding or cover other than that in which it is published and without a similar condition including this condition being imposed on the subsequent purchaser.

First published in 2024 by Gatehouse Press,
an imprint of Story Machine.

130 Silver Road
Norwich
NR3 4TG
United Kingdom

www.storymachines.co.uk

Set in IM FELL Double Pica Pro; used under licence.

Printed and bound in the UK by 4Edge

All the characters in this book are fictitious, and any resemblance to actual persons, living or dead, is purely coincidental.

For Victor, without whom this book (and my happiness) would not have been possible.

It: Who's this I hear, ringing like the tiny bell in a nut?
Who's there, squealing like an early bud?

        (Sea, be quiet a while)

Go on,
I'm listening.

The Ghost of Wuffa, King of the Angles

In which Wuffa considers then addresses the land of his kingdom, East Anglia, circa 575.

a hed growing bak its tung
wer hovels slipped into,
as lyke the lowse creeps in
a softened shu,

wher,
huddled agaynst befor-bristle,
huddled agaynst yet-bulk,
both as blank as chalk,
they trubble me still.

a breething beest, I swet me in
who, lyke the Fen, fills a hol to cuvver it
with welling ox-reek, unyons, werked gold.

aghast me not
yu wher, who, tho swollowed
remain un-eeten,
diving in th'erth like a weed.

scorn not my hevvy tred
yu sprowt, yu snayk-in-a-hol,
yu allredy carving arrow,
and stop not, my hart, too offen.

Flint

In which Flint *is formed, discovered, and worked into the buildings of the city of Norwich.*

I am a dark clodling deep inside the coddling sea,
thick with drifts of tiny dead: fish, gribkin, sponge.
Cheek and jowl a soupy seeping is I,
a lulled, dull clump and wondrous lumpish,
quiet, secrety.

Hush, now the wash spits me up
on this gritty shore of scrapings, gullbone, otherstone.
Strange, strange, strange this sun-thing;
I have a back now, for it can dry and scorch and flake
to little ashes.

The surf behind me laughs;
night then day then night pass and I am mad.

Then, in the bright time, standing on two legs
the wormlings have come in roughen wools,
with their smells, their crunchy gull-talk.
The wormlings come with hands,
they thieve me right away. They

take
        take
                take.

When struck, my dun eye hatches,
split flash of fire flying,
like a black mare that stamps to a halt at midnight,
like a wyvern maw yawing sparks,
I drop scraps of dragon, moonflakes, sudden, quick, uncatched.

Behold, my scalped insides, knapped, hulled, unblinking,

are a scoop and jag of glaucous glass.
The wormlings have pummeled me to slick, slicing bits
all while cursing and devilling, splitting fingers.
I am a glut of cuttings, tinier, manyer, otherer.

       I did not know of what I was until they had me,
       and now they have me. A bile, I think.

Now they go weasel-rooting, make chaff my chalk,
they sniff me out, these dry gribkins,
bore through my buried bodling, hole-riddling,
haul me up, heft me out, a hobnail from a wormcast.
Then all me spies the strangeness here.

The land of the wormlings is barrenous flat,
not one good stone to stand upon another.
They say I am to shrive it of its emptiness:
kirks to prick the sky and let their godling in,
a tall wall to ring their skinny living.

       They shall be born in me,
       shall sleep and shit and die in me.

Sly work, I rise in strange shape,
I rise in the vast flatness of this watery land
brim with sunset, with lapwing shrieking.
I rise roundly in towers, a girding of grey-black milky eye caps,
or I rise square-cut, flush and grim-sit, like king-teeth.

Queer it is, queer to be here,
land of quiet, waving rushes,
of green and orange and gold.
I too am prettious queer,
am like none other.

       I become old.

These wormlings,

kranzy hoodlums, frothing biters spectre-making.
The teary plooshes run down my gullet as vinegar,
vinegar stripping. They explode,
they burn and riot like summer grass and are killed.

Listen: coins chequery clicking, wet thumps,
witches skulkily, dancing bells, fork-and-pitch-snarl,
gold and prayernoise, hell and prayernoise, ale and prayernoise,
booms in the night. Last of autumn's sweet apple cider,
spilt and unlike.

See: wormlings, shut and dreaming of
a fine, scaled leviathan, spiked with flecks of flame.
Their cats creep among the mother-die,
forget-me-not, death-come-quickly, a happy
lamby gambol, then brick and flesh bits, my shim shaking.

And all that love business, all melty stutter,
all ranked up shivering like arrowheads,
like wheat when the combine comes. They moan
in the dark corners of me. They go one into the other
like rain into the bluebell, or wither, stiff sudden squalls all.

They have carved cracks in me to fall in,
a pit in me to be thrown in, a gaol in me to rot in,
a dole office to go mad in. I stench. I stench.
There are crook-toothed wraiths shuffling in me,
rubbing a divot in, dying of cold in me.

Strange pinky-browny paws, madder'd, urine'd, yessir'd,
lifes tucked as eggs. Tiny wierdlings, bunch of poets,
they yell all which way, wrens with the lids blown off.
How stand it? Rampant sick these matchsticks, a swarm
of unnings barely born but sparking.

How they love the heavy purple flower in spring,
how they candle-carol in the dark-cold and starving,
how kiss, how cast each other out, how lie down to ruin,

how become wet when it rains. Their ghosts they blow by me
and sigh and cross like a lost valentine.

Swine-stuck pearls, these bitsy monsters,
and have made a plush pillow of me
for all the tender heads, smeared and snuffed.
Why so sorrowing weak? Where are you all going?
Get back here, filthy treasure!

They are my pebble babes, not yet dust.
Then they are dust, my dust babes, briefly pebbles.

Tie a cord about you,
tie a red cord that you will all return to me.
Always to bed they go, to ground, to grass,
my little loves they pour through this, my boxy bodkin,
a gout of sharp stars.

Then, in the far-off, I see *It*,
amble-padding, jaunty-like and tongue-loll,
full black and eye current-red
as if all time were at *Its* heel,
and at *Its* heel, the sea.

*My love, I wander wide and wild
and travel 'tween the willow,
while my love, you weep and sigh,
the loosestrife gay and yellow.*

*Your girl may wend her way to thee,
a drake might dance upon a tine;
that which is was what shall be
and all that shall be fine.*

River Wensum

In which the river Wensum sings a song, passes through the city, and recalls its history, from New Mills Yard to its confluence with the Yare

pip

      pup

            pap

   pitter

      pattery

            slippery
        trickley

     crisherly
         crasherly
     blathery
        thundery

       R

       A

      I

       N

I wrinkle like treacle winking,
    like the nose of that woman running
with a satchel raised above her head
    and her hair several whips.
        She ducks, I'm goosed.
    And who might you be, gandering?

What was that? Forgetful?
    As the tadpole forgets its tail,
always seeping salubriously from the chalk,
shallow then very deep, wound about a reed, asleep,
    back again,
        with a satchel raised above my head.

  R   I
     A   N

Down here, creeping at creature level,
    all bestirred by fowl invention,
the barbel makes a small hump,
    in a knot of mint, the cygnet;
beneath is smooth as a bubble
    whence I come, rippling, solemn

        round and round,
            round and round and round again

    You think me wistful?
  What I think of you I'll never tell
and never told Kemp neither, that prancing tool
    had hair flung like several whips to lick
this city's knot of weirdness.
    This city: whelp, pike, peeling bell, cute-ugly duck

        round and round,
            round and round and round again

Once, I crept from the ice, singing,
    stippling myself with green, gathering,
passing through the stiff dark, flinty, murmurous,
    the moon it spun like a turbine. Then the city
was there, surprised, then the city was being built,
then the city was dead, the workmen removed their shirts.

    When I whistled the city came trotting,

                        I bristled with froglets, would make a wet wife
                to the city, sweet, queer, the barbel
                        made a small hump. I shuttled refuse, product,
                delinquents, suicides, would go, would come, would come.
                        The workmen removed their shirts.

R

   A

I

   N

                It's coming back to me, is still coming.
Pitter pattery and who might you be, gandering?
                I was just dreaming a fine dream, blent with a song
more quiet than the inside of a fish. You, you're still wet
                behind the ears, look at you, listening.
                        What, would you translate for me?

                turn about your aural shell the buddleia sticks
                        in winter pricking, the red bricks' lonesome dripplet,
                transpose in your shuttered brain, flashing
                        like a magpie, the one who bends?
                I bent gladly to the mill owner's knee
                        for good flour and cheap,

entered sweetly the bellies of my people
        as darkness enters the guts of a thief.
When The Abbot of St Benets, and Wetherby (a bastard)
        made to leash me to his own mills
snatch me from the table, clutch me close and legal,
        a private death with public corpses,

                        Robert Toppes, merchant, tore the common seal
                                from the Guild hall, the crowd piled wood against
                the Cathedral gates, threatened to burn the priory

and kill the monks. And John Gladman rode
through the city on a horse, dressed like a king in crown,
scepter and sword. 24 more also on horseback

with crowns and carrying bows and arrows,
along with 100 followers, and by the loud
ringing of bells were able to gather 3000 people.
The Mayor and others, so-called Rysers
ageynst the King, summarily fyned, and a weapon
of The Abbot against the good people of Norwich

                                            R   I
                                                A   N

R   I
   A   N

Where was I? Sliding under little Coslany
    bridge like a damp cat

        by the old flint church, which one day
           is confused to find itself
                a school for acrobats

                sliding under merry iron Coslany
                          bridge

should you see a man here, should you see
    his red left hand and his red right hand
flensed like, a dyer man, a madder man, let's call him
    Jack, Jack Red. Should you see him here
on a Thursday noon, with his pipe, with his wife
    at home, should you see this man,

        this is my man.

        Look, here he is.
        'Jack? Jack Red?'

Jack Red stares into the Wensum and spits

'Jack Red, Jack Red

are you so dead as not
to hear me purring here or
comb my fingers through my hair?

Jack Red, Jack Red

I'll sing each star by name
and swallow them, I'll sing you
to your grave, then out again

Jack Red, Jack Red

In summer, with naked foot,
then calf, then thigh, men like you
would bend to me and sigh'

Jack Red: 'river bleeds like a pig'

'Jack Red,

Yesterday my last frog crawled from me,
dead, like a strawberry.
You didn't call it 'dye' for nothing, Jack.

Jack Red, I am all a bitten tongue

I would sweep you down, hold you to my bed
would feed you a silver fish.
I've fed you, Jack, haven't I?'

Jack Red: 'there's 'bell. Back to work.'

'That's a new bell,
and a new Master, Jack.

Can't you hear Him?
Like a thief entering the guts of the dark
he brings his new machines,
his new concoctions, his new world

and no narrow cot in it
for you, Jack -
no songbird, no stalk of grass.

The bell of St Miles Coslany is ringing

500 years a dyer,
500 years I shuttled a tonnage
of fine, expensive death,
refuse, product,
delinquents, suicides.

Would you be gathered, Jack?
Would you lie down quiet in his loud lap,
and when he strikes you, Jack,
would you no longer cry,
but like the barbel,
make a small hump?

No, not *my* Jack.

I have got clear of you,
my love, at last.'

Jack Red knocks out his pipe and leaves

RAIN
        RAIN
    GO   *AWAY*
              COME AGAIN
                        ONE DAY TO STAY
        pip
            pap

pup

look,
slapped on the old Eastern Electric building,   vandals
a looming gasbag, anarcho-communist   most probably

> *[We made no inquiries after monsters,*
> *than which nothing is more common]*

one expectoration of whitewash
the drear reflection hoarding my back,
letters like   a crowd of whitefly

> *[There is a great number*
> *of noblemen among you]*

from here, taxis on the Charing Cross   road
merge with cyclist flesh
a pub slips names   like nooses

> *[that are themselves idle as drones,*
> *that subsist on other men's labour]*

who put that there? hard to   make it out
can't quite call to mind

> *[Whom, to raise their revenues,*
> *they pare to the quick]*

a red stump of pigeon foot,
the squat where cherry pink punks   go to kiss
cops or a bad smell following

> *[Even to the point of beggaring themselves]*

old youth
and nasty attitudes,   I wouldn't

[Indeed, nature has so made us,
that we all love to be flattered]

there's a ringing   in my ear
must be water in it

[and to please ourselves with our own notions:
the old crow loves his young]

this dumb text, it itches   like a skin
like some industrial   unpleasantness

[Ill masters]

the cat-black night,
a flicked   burning
tangerine cigarette   circle

[It is a vain thing to boast your severity in punishing]

she worked in a silver shop
in the mall for minimum wage

[As if it were to his advantage that his people
have neither riches nor liberty]

why bother with script   disastering itself?
on such matters   I couldn't say

[whereas necessity and poverty blunts them,
makes them patient, beats them down,]

frying pan/fire, pot/kettle/black, strike/iron
or some other such   nonsense

[and breaks that height of spirit]

head collapsing into tail   again

and again

> *[He could not keep his subjects in their duty
> but by oppression and ill usage,]*

did you ever see a snake swim in me?

> *[and by rendering them poor and miserable]*

no one ever believes it   when they see it,
but they never   forget it

> *[Being thus mutilated
> in the service of their king and country]*

the building is still standing
years later by whatever   indifferent
stupidity

> *[Some forced sense will be put on them]*

but I wouldn't know a thing about that

> *[I must freely own
> that as long as there is any property,
> while money is the standard
> of all other things,]*

gossip is that thing
we are not   short of

> *[I cannot think that a nation can be governed
> either justly or happily]*

some things just fall, like an unlucky man
ankle over neck

> *[And by these means, this your island,*

which seemed as to this particular

down and down

> *the happiest in the world,*
> *will suffer much by the cursed avarice*
> *of a few persons]*

an upturned crust
scab-grey, wet-bloated
best not ask			nor tell

> *[A man must barefacedly approve*
> *of the worst counsels and consent to the blackest designs]*

why must I be always looking up
at something's face?

> *[All I could be able to do*
> *would be to preserve myself from being mad,*

slack-jawed, gawping

> *while I endeavored to cure*
> *the madness of others]*

sometimes I think

> *[Manage things with all the dexterity in your power,*
> *so that if you are not able to make them go well,]*

damn them,

> *[they may be as little ill as possible; for,*
> *except all men were good,]*

damn them all,

[everything cannot be right]

guts *and* eyes

*[Perhaps better for you, not to engage
in so ridiculous a contest with a fool]*

slip under, along,

[How deaf would they be to all I could say!]

away

*[As, in aftertimes perhaps,
it will be forgot by our people that I was ever there]*

*that which is was what shall be
and all that shall be fine.*

Listen, the   R
                    A
          I
                N

Pap

    Pup

Pip

What is that place, up ahead,
beyond the Duke Street bridge?
A someone there, I think I know, mouthing –

"Spring is a cat that wants to come in,
'Let the cat in, please.'
I'd like to tell you something:
you are drinking tea in the garden of The Playhouse Bar,
your mug has a picture of a pink dinosaur,

tomorrow it will be a recipe for mushroom soup.
Look, here come the leaves
on the big, over-leaning trees,
they are like animals that must be coaxed.
The danger of a late frost still stalks about,
even now in the mind of a leaf.
Lime green moss, hunkering on a low, red brick wall,
remembers that frost,
then gets back on with its being lowly.
Why should I feel this way,
as if a red brick wall ought to miss me
after a long, regretful absence?
Would it rather miss the old dog there,
who crosses his paws and whistles?
His misty breath is not unlike the misty breath of tea.
You are drinking a beer and the yellow echinaceas
flex their bright button heads,
the hydrangea a slow collision of pink puff balls.
Such things are absorbed by those other things
with the strength to accommodate them,
like the grimace someone has drawn on the fence there,
Cheshire-style, below two knots for eyes.
Every day it becomes less unsettling
and more complicated.
Then the big trees they clatter
and cast their bouncy, bending shadows.
You are drinking a coke. The taste of coke
is like autumn light, solemn and syrupy,
and like that light it needles one
with flashes of abject romance
and its bronziness.
The garden is a scampering hajj of leaves,
damp, like something one desires to fall into,
but from which some day one will return,
smarter, braver, and less vain.
Do you think anyone can be truly good?
Yes, in fact I do. Was that a stupid thing to say?
Perhaps, when winter is about to come

in its nudity and cleanliness, with its absolute of blue.
I can feel the dumb moss trembling on its wall.
What a thing, like when the phone rings
too early or too late to be anything good.
Chains of coloured lights are coming on, it gets dark
early now, orange goodbying the friendly shapes of things.
The doleful cat eyes of spring."

       Pup

   Pip

            Pap

             What was that?

The city is dead, the city is built, the workmen
   remove their shirts. Are you still watching,
      my ganderer? Perchance have glimpsed
   my belly slowly roll, ale bottle brown,
to stroke the willow's querulous tress, perchance
     a flash of underthings, succulent as cress.

     Gander longer, translate for me the peeling
   cathedral bell. Hours are dropping like small
      sad stones. On the green, they come, they go
   litter and leaves, wind and snow. He's there again,
     that guy who stands on Blackfriar's Bridge
singing folk ballads. *Are you going to Scarborough*

Fair? Let no man steal your thyme. To tell
   the truth, I like that guy, his body is like
     a soft, tired chair, his face like bristles of frost
   on a fencepost. But the singing I can do without -
a jowl-shaking shriek all down St George's Street,
   in the art school, up Friar's Quay, like cats, bats

     round and round,

                                    round and round and round again

            it goes, my wetter than woman heart, and frailer
and weaker, and faints, and spits and boils away
            when it faces fire's blazing. I recall Elm Hill was blazing,
the cobbles baked underfoot, fire he leapt through the air
            like a tyger, Hell had quit his caverns to bray
and snap and throw his hands up from the thatch.

Two days and a night it cooked away the dark,
            red and yellow, the stench scalded nostrils, the noise
of falling beams crashed in upon the sleepless
            like a shout upon a dream, and every place
from the lay sisters' house to St Simon and St Jude
            was a black runnel, was smoking, gone,

            and with it 360 of my cyte's houses, all brent to ash,
not a drop among me with the strength to dowse it.
            Pittery pattery, my cyte came back to me, in timber,
tile and glass, it bred again its well-respected men,
            and all their gold, it stooped and sagged and again
was old and crackles with history's rumoring

                        round and round,
                                    round and round and round again

pelargoniums pour, hot and brief
below Fye bridge, cool your grief

            R
            A
            I
            N   R
                     A
                     I
                     N   R
                              A
                              I

N

WARNING: shallow water

          palms flat   belly splayed   tapeworm I
I, I unsatisfy   no archeology   what colour am I?
what gender?   no taste   no odor   who sluicely slips the loop,

the collar   and drops through any open hand   call me wasteland   call me slim   anorexic   shrinking into sand   ill I fit, ill I fit   wherever
can be found

      through my chink of eye   I see you, ganderer   promenading feet
where willows weep   you ought to know   all water is the same water there is only
      one of me   when the sky is blue   I am too

    and the long song of fronds   the trills of rippleous trickles   is the old song

of solitude:

Kett, my Kett
upon this bank he sat
when they tore down the bridge to town
and around each of us alone
closed the box
that would never again be opened

     pip

         pup

        pap

              How's that? The mill,
                    what happened to its carnage crash?
                        its terror hammer, hand mangle,
                  mother bash? All I hear is manager tongue
        reaching like a leech, a piss-thin thing, mad

as a pencil prick, as a weasel's eye, in secret withering.

But through that measly aperture, despite itself,
    comes surging:

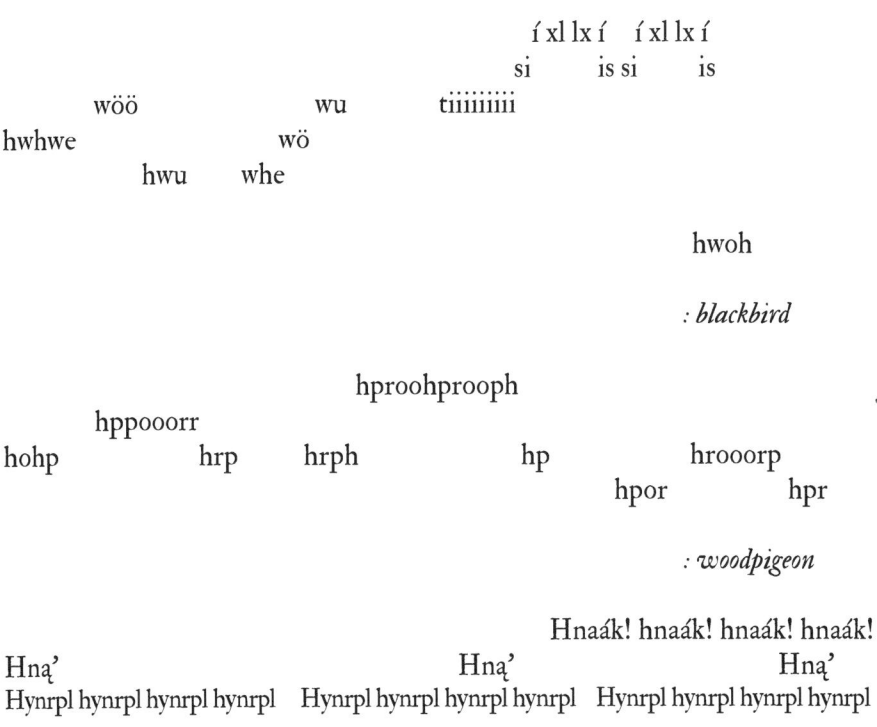

                                í xl lx í   í xl lx í
                            si   is si   is
   wöö   wu   tiiiiiiiii
hwhwe   wö
     hwu   whe

                               hwoh

                               : blackbird

               hproohprooph
   hppooorr
hohp   hrp   hrph   hp   hrooorp
                         hpor   hpr

                       : woodpigeon

                  Hnaák! hnaák! hnaák! hnaák!
Hną'   Hną'   Hną'
Hynrpl hynrpl hynrpl hynrpl Hynrpl hynrpl hynrpl hynrpl Hynrpl hynrpl hynrpl hynrpl

                       : ducks

protruding turret tapering towards the top
11.2 meters across, 14.6 metres high and
divided into 3 stories, quatrefoil gunports
in the lower levels for both hand cannons
and crossbows with overlapping fields of fire
higher than the parapets forming a look out
position, roof reinforced with large timber
joints for supporting the heavier bombards
possibly on wheeled carriages, specialised artillery
initially used as offensive siege weapons to

deal with an external threat, one of several
fortifications capable of suppressing attackers
1.8 metres thick at the base, with a core of flint
stone plinth and several layers of mortared flint
and was well-furnished, 36,850 bricks, stone,
sand, lime, a hoist and various equipment, at least
170 cartloads of stone, twice the listed number
purchased, both prestigious and practical, designed
to maintain a garrison when required, was faced
on inside and out with various putlog holes as
brick better absorbed the impact of artillery fire
a team of gunners by 1355, and by 1385 had 50
gunpowder pieces controlling access to the waterway
erected a circuit of defensive stone walls and ditches
a protective timber palisade, the tower's considerable
height crenelated with 9 wide embrasures, particularly
well-executed, the earliest known and finest brickwork
in all of England, ground and second floor had fireplaces
first and second also having garderobes, chasing and
sockets, and was earlier known as The Dungeon
two rebel attacks, the only equivalents in the country
which he turned on the Tower, damaging the latter's
parapets as the city industrialised, erosion from the
river soon caused extensive damage: wide splits formed
up and down, floors and roof lost, only a shell, however
avoiding destruction by 1378 lapsed into ruinous condition

black slats flash between green leaves
a bull tilts the swell of his head

sky blushes, catching herself in the open barrel
tiny crescent moon a stud in her ear

inside, the reed vibrates
humming a note:

> *My love, I wander wide and wild*
> *and travel 'tween the willow,*

while my love, you weep and sigh,
the loosestrife gay and yellow.

Your girl may wend her way to thee,
a drake might dance upon a tine;
that which is was what shall be
and all that shall be fine.

R A I N

round and round,
      round and round and round again

The moon is spinning like a turbine,
      the city seeps from the chalk,
the city makes a small hump,
      the city is dead,
workman, remove your shirt,
      thief of the dark.

        Wait, the green is leaning in, and rain
     stings my back with its suspicious chat
          me spooling along stone alone -
                this must be Bishop Bridge.

Leave me, Kett.
    You see him, don't you ganderer,
with the rope around his neck?
    Leave me, you and your mound of 20,000 rebel men
fixed in the shape of a hill where the prison is.
    Leave off your bulged fool's eyeballs, damn you.

         And there, you see them, ganderer? Behind him
            heretics spilling over a pit, staked Lollards
       spitting candle fat, their skeletons flashing from the flesh,
              dead as thinking in the bucket of the head.
          Go! Off with you! This city,
              it's a restless bone mill, red itching,

rebel dyed red in the wool
scratching at its red welts
foxed red, wilder than fever and fire
them like bores, like burrs, keen as spikes
as the snap of the camel's back
must be something in the water
some finger of hot iron
that dibs the glisten of their eyes
some coal that plunks in a steaming arc of piss
some mustard seeping from the grave hole
some trickle into baby's bottle
some red spider sitting in it
water on the brain's griddle
some drip some lick
in the bloodstream
some blood fish and bone
fish lodged in the bone
bone fishing out the blood
bloody bone deep with fish
thicker than water blood
flow bones
flow blood
like fish
rise
rise
whelm
burn
flood

    Don't you go telling me how bread is not the body of Christ, too late, I'm slipping away in the form of a green and silent pike

    [the cathedral bell is ringing]

    What is this place?
    Since when did this errant blue bugloss populate?
    Since when was the garden washed in flowers' white, rampant froth?

I suspect this is June...and I'm a still pool stopped under a swan.
I feel...I feel stuffed with gravel and lead, a phantom limb

[the cathedral bell is ringing]

stumping. They built something here. Through that arch
I carried...you would never think anything could be so heavy.
It's somewhere, a faint alarm I fail to find...
with no eyes to search...no shoulder to shunt...
whatever it was I lost...brushing air with fingerless...what

[the cathedral bell is ringing]

am I doing here? This is a heavy place,
like a stopped clock, like a voice only just too low to hear,
just between the green-shadow of the full, trailing trees.
Someone is shouting up ahead, traffic, gulls;
slew towards, on, away, up the middle, gone.

Two banks beyond Foundry Bridge

same shit, new diseases
e.g. emotional destruction
a sliced gravitational stem
being locked in one's personal egg
never getting born
but we're all in the same boat
aren't we
GDP sluicing over your head
between your feet
well, what's wrong with Nando's
it's fucking good
rubble. oil. guts. glass. input
be happy, be happy as loudly
as possible, going forward, yeh
unreasonable emotions
well, of fucking course
the skyline zapping up and down

flats only serial killers could live in
little bits of turf outside, shrubbery
nice actually, good area, historic like
benches, couchspace
someone's cousin's place
from industrial concerns
to leisure pursuits
cranes, piles of black slag
a dilating lung, seagulls
i.e. your grandad's day
saxons, black death
that sort of thing
nice. fun. ecstatic even.
Timothy Randall Martin, you're a hole
Queen of Iceni, well shit, Tim
step into any Frankie & Benny's
come out of another
it's the future, Tim. Imagine it
all chain restaurants
nodes in collapsed space, brilliant
nationalise Frankie & Benny's
perfect the technology
our rodent hearts battering
til arrest, states of excitement
check the condition of the city's liver
check for yellow tinges in its eyes
point to where it hurts
who can point to where it hurts
repeat, no one is hurting you
I can't remember why I'm angry
but at least it's a job, yeh
gaps in the sentences
filling with traffic
with undeveloped space
the sentence becoming
increasingly more difficult to say
the road back to the sentence
has fewer pedestrian crossings

the sentence is noise and
understandably catastrophic
to the ear. the future
crashing up the lanes
at Hollywood Bowl
flow, like water
like change, yeh

                                  The architect drives in a pole and splits
                         a metaphorical amphora that hereto had tipped
                      and singly decanted time, now darkening city limits
                                 with red, gouting, diamond-hard liquid.

                             So, ardourous and lapped by confluences,
                         posterity peeps through dereliction's hedge:
                  hoardings, haphazard, tell us what insouciance is,
while new developments managerially authorise an edge,

                    each construction's current shows its rate of flow
                      and in their wrecks' decaying prove the mettle
                        of denser bones below, bones, on inspection
                           stripped of living's precious prattle.

                        The pastel egg of any olden place, hatching
                  in the future the gorgeous, paradisal bird of past,
             we turn over to find it long ago eaten, matching
this, nobody's voice, describing in air what we imagined last.

        RAIN   RAIN   RAIN   RAIN   RAIN

              RAIN   RAIN   RAIN   RAIN

        RAIN   RAIN   RAIN   RAIN   RAIN

                          RAIN

RAIN   RAIN
RAIN

That sound above us,
      I thought it was a high ball of thunder
dropping along and down the black,
      pachinko sky. 27,359 people are shouting
in the stadium, and riding storm gusts, their voice
      tinges the giant air here and there

with disappointment, ecstasy,
      confusion. Minor tone, major, it's playing
          its scale, listen. It follows. Slink now,
I'm tired, ganderer. The mist down here
      is scented with mint and vinegar.
          Who put out the factories' eyes?

What has scraped them clean off the earth?
      Is this the surface of the moon?
Then the moon is tugging on a shift of green
      to hide her nakedness. But the train's straight line
heart still ticker tacks, through moss and scrub I duck

      my head under the tracks and sense
I slide towards some kind of death. A stranger
      is walking calmly alongside, small, scant, it travels
          'tween the willow while all around, the loosestrife
      blooming gay and yellow

Wensum
    wend   sum
    when   dew   runs
               sun   unwed
               wherry nude
    why   weary   new
                      wear   dawn
                            awe   are

```
            aware
                away
                a yaw    yarn
                              yearn   ear
                                      year
                                      Yare
                                              Yare
                                                      Yare
```

It: And what of *me,* Wensum. What have you to say about *me?*
Wensum:
It: I know you're there. Who couldn't hear your droning?
Wensum:
It: Very well. But listen, someone is talking about me.

Black Shuck

A block of yellow light drops from the doorway of The Adam and Eve *like a churchyard slab, from inside float two male voices, Grandfather Reeve and Young John Reeve. The summer air is acrid with petunias gone to rot.*

Mark now,

whoso hears *Its* wind-suck gaol of crying
one night, on some road alone in the brackish black,
whoso's organs soft *It* fingers with far-off near-mistaken moan
like a grieving woman in her age,
already *It* licks the cockles of his eyes
and laps the kidney from his side,

for no church, no priory keeps that man
nor bars *It* fast away, for God nor Devil is *Its* master,
nor closes that single, searching, bursted eye
nor shuts the mouth that tar-like slavers,
nor stays *Its* door-pounding paws, their booming scrape,
nor saves the marked ear its taste of coming sorrow

> *curse Its name boy, must y'never*
> *say your prayers boy, must y'ever*

It slips from lightening's crack like an eel,
It spurts, porter black from a cloud that's rent by thunder,
and in heavy rain *It* hides *Its* footsteps, soft, fast,
padding, padding, ever padding right behind,
horse-huge, clergy-clever, *It*
blood-stinking, stirs the sibilant rush with silent breath

and don't you think *It* just some cur, some whelp, some bitch,
and don't you think *It* won't come softly,
in fair scheming shape - there creeps from the wet dark
your own sweet mother, your smiling girl, your ginger tom
come curled about your ankle, one eye red as madder,

and don't you think *It* won't speak fair

> *tempt Its prowling, must y'never*
> *sing your hymns boy, must y'ever*

'Is that you, John Reeve, my darling man?'
say 'yes' and *It* unzips your bowels to froth and bilge
upon the ground, trammels them up, sucks them down,
It tears the darling face from young John Reeve, his empty
nose a gawking hole, *It* plucks his brains and scatters them,
the restful ground would not hide the blood of young John Reeve

say 'no', *Its* jaw droops long and wide, *Its* tongue wags
to catch John Reeve, then the ground it yawns
and all afire his young skin burns, his fat bubbles
before his own popping eyes, *It* pulls John down
where none have risen, where all forget and are forgotten
and an unloved nothingness is John

> *laugh at phantoms must y'never*
> *hide your sins boy, must y'ever*

and should John give no answer?

> *if'n still he thinks him clever,*
> *thrice damn his foolish soul forever*

> *The clink of two half-pint glasses is swept away on the darkness, where it is snatched up by a listening, pointed ear.*

It: Such lies. Don't you think, Wensum?
Wensum:
It: Until later then -

> *My love, I wander wide and wild*
> *and travel 'tween the willow,*
> *while my love, you weep and sigh,*
> *the loosestrife gay and yellow.*

Julian of Norwich

In which St Julian of Norwich, for the first time, transcribes the divine love of God into English.

I was aroused to agitation again,
Him saying *after* and saying *all*
but never *against*,
as absolute and abrupt as a button.
A baby was bawling,
and my bonnet had been battered by the breeze
when between my bare hands,
a beetle crawled across the cushion and clung,
then the clear Spring cried:
'Chiffchaff, cockchafer, chamomile!'
Could I, couldn't I, in my discomfort,
have done differently,
in those doldrums that were death,
which are without daffodil, without dandelion?
No. For despair is deeper than death,
but delight's deeper still.
For example: the elegance of eggs,
of everything easily caressed
and everything else, less easily caressed
i.e. the perfect evening egg
which is the sun eliding with the sea,
and where they meet we feel it, fearfully, effusively.
If...if I fail?
Fifty, five hundred, five thousand failures,
but of love? Infinity.
Of love, those friendly, female phonemes: *forever*.
Furthermore: fur, fish scales, frogspawn,
fungus, fingers, the ferrous rust on the garden gate
and other such graces,
they give me the good grief again.
How good it is to be a grain in the glove of God,
how good to be the ghost in his hand,

no bigger than a hazelnut.
Here are endless heavens heaped as hay bales,
and the horizon a hopscotch for the hammering heart.
Inside I hear His hissing, uninhibited,
incendiary, it itches, I just...
just knock me down with a kingcup.
        Like lifting the lid on a field of millet,
the word 'moon' one night in May,
nascent, nacreous,
will be no more nor less than love,
will be none other than
only ordinary.
How I was over, how I was out,
I was an odd odour, I had gone off, but
I was not overcome.
Love, like the pop of a peapod, painful,
precisely placed, it had a petal-quality,
piquant, unpicking quiet doubt.
I quiesced to it, as the quince quiesces to the palm,
no quarrel, no qualm.
        I turn round that rare afternoon,
remembering red, then redder still,
and a residue that resisted reason: slowly,
sure as sugar and shale, the shroud of time
unwinding under His thimbled thumb.
Undo, unravel, veer away,
unmake it very well,
so all shall be well
and all manner of things
shall be made well,
shall be made exactly *yes*,
exactly those dazzling spaces
after z.

Norwich Cathedral

The voice of Norwich Cathedral wells up from its root at the tomb of Thomas Gooding once every hour

You who *were*, like a curtain faintly parted, like the mute, vexing dark behind,
mere outline, once a creature of this digesting earth, a melancholy ligature becoming
solid, fluttering under the pin of a moment's brightness, the dote of prodigal Time,
rush onward now, mortify ground's jealous claw, spite the wind's inconstancy, you'll go
full clear of mortal tether, rarer than particles of air, and though you might dissemble,
find yourself in fearful Future's shallow hand, ended, you are not in truth,
so says I who tolls the time and tolls the time and tolls the time
so says I who tolls the time and tolls the time and tolls the time
find yourself in fearful Future's shallow hand, ended, you are not in truth
full clear of mortal tether, rarer than particles of air, and though you might dissemble,
rush onward now, mortify ground's jealous claw, spite the wind's inconstancy, you'll
go solid, fluttering under the pin of a moment's brightness, the dote of prodigal Time,
mere outline, once a creature of this digesting earth, a melancholy ligature becoming
you who *were*, like a curtain faintly parted, like the mute, vexing dark behind.

Fen

The fen as always, speaks

now you see me. out dug rows to spook. line and up. the broad flat furrow. now you. black converging curve. sliced. twinkling. don't.

pocket. hide and. remain alive. brimful of knot. carefully depositing. brown soundless future. soup enough to suffocate. gems repeating under.

not you. demolished. this long glottis of God. and be fleas in the mud. who? is kneeling. never or. what? gargantuan. bendful. me.

as above so. longest noughts quill. down and touch twin. cold pool of mirrors. with high warbler. widest wisped cheek. emptiness. below.

debridled. uncounted jewels the flowers. bow then dance. damsels black and blue. shapes of heat. with cool flung spark. call all who's flesh and living.

peekaboo. hairs of my head. for swallow. water's lurk crack flashing. will softest vanish. slough hunter. eat air. green your foot and gone.

had drained me dark. I'm walking. at low field. did blind scrape sky's hand. shrink stars. invisible rattling. a dry skin of rage. haunt dragon. fly.

William of Norwich

1144, *the body of William, 12, is found in Thorpe wood, mutilated and gagged with a wooden teasel. What follows next is a shadow, incorrigible and mute, upon the city of Norwich.*

The People

Rafty weather when we saw him
puce and blue,
the prick of his eye, a bishy-barney-bee,
his mouth all burst with ha and hacker,
an erriwiggle crawling
from his titty-totty ear. And still,
those hedge-betties would not quit
their unchristian mardle -
her blaring, terrible; we knew her,
the mother like a wet rag, sopping.

There's none among us made of stones,
none who do not count the hairs on every head
nor wince when plucked.
Wretches lie none, nor lie down,
no matter how thacked,
how left duddering in the smur,
left duddering on the rim
of the lord's pretty gate, knocking
on his swaddled Jewry.

Let me not higgle nor barter,
nor be turned, a duzzy fool away again.
Dead boys tell no tales, nor us neither,
nor haven't known the snake
aslept in the baby's bed
from that first flashing of his clever tooth.

Jesus God, bring me a spike for winkling,
to pick and drag the soft, fat fact
from all its haunts and hidings,
for there is no gold in all my ken
to rinse the clag of boy-blood.
Look you, in our eye,
we dast you, talk your slaver and squit.

Joseph Ben Solomon of Norwich

What mother, for three shillings, trades her son
to a stranger? She should have named a higher price.
Unless, he was truly worth so little.
Why now be aggrieved of the sale?
And why, when done, would we toss him in the wood,
some miles from our sumptuous, well-appointed homes?
I would choose the river, as easy as tossing a stone.
And why gag his screaming with a teasel, the labour of which
is so foreign to our small, softened hands?
Wads of silk and strings of jewels are all so much the nearer.
O, but it must have been a Jew,
for no Christian could submit to such indulgences.
And if it were one Jew, well it must have been all,
being, as we know, a single body of convoluted machination,
not like good Christian souls, each unique,
a slick, quick-witted star.

Babble!
Should the Nazarene stride into town today, pissing purest light,
they'd think they spy a barbed tail peeping from his skirt
and a hoof inside each sandal.
They would straight away dismember him, like dogs,
as bloody as their brains are dull, and still they'll crow
that they know evil, as well they know their own selves.
One will never see such misers as these, who, for want
of wealth to hoard, begrudge each and every clemency,
and call it good.

I may say what I like, though it scalds the tongue to say it.
Speech is nothing when the hearer hears only the merry tune
of his invention, when his spirit is decided on loathing,
and all that is said he twists to the same foul confluence.

Or is this grief?
Is this grief that cooks a mind prior crackled by privations,
sorrows row on row like furrows behind the plough,
like leaves that sweep beneath a draughty door,
and in a fragile pile, stay there? Look at them,
vagrants in this gilded world
and would the black streets incarnadine if only
one among them might hurl a single spear of light,
strike, and for that moment, be happy.
It is a charm against that snake, the sharp-toothed Truth.

Norwich, you wear a colourful shroud and sigh
with more restless dybbuks than William, bless the child.
Leaning in, one hears the sound of minds snapping,
like birds atwitter below the chamber windows of one's days.
Louder, louder. Look, I am shaking.
How bright they grow, see them coming
with all their retinue, with their parsimonious souls.
It is so silent I might hear my garden rose crushed
by a soft, stealthy boot. It would not even wake my daughter -

Enough, to bed!
Do I not sleep at the foot of a king, and of England no less?
Do I not have his ear as he has my purse? As he has me?
Birds fly and leaves scatter, the furrow fills up with grass.
See, already this business passes, foolish fancies live not long.
To bed, to bed! Let such worries not twist and squirm
but be tossed in the pit of dream instead.

The People

a teasle slitting fine slivers of his tongue
               to wet bladderwrack his gums
               tortured, therefore
no nonicking, hoolly,
but has sly craft in it
               queering art, and singular
devilry, certain
and need we remind
the night were Passover?
               brains gone fosey, green and blue
               wouldn't add the two, and see
               as a maid saw William
in a Jews' house that very night,
through a chink in the door
               their secrets, disgorging
               as well she'd know, pampling there
               the sheriff, he gurned at that
bribed then
where money is, lies are,
               and Jew's work evidenced
so this be deep as ditches
for fying out, I dast
               and William not the first
nor last, as says that convert Theobald
               who was a Jew, so knows, and saw
               with the skin of his own eyeballs
their reasty laws, the lots drawn:
which coven to huddle close in golden halls
and kill a Christian?
               and this year it fell to Norwich, and us
               to us their nasty magics
               ritual gouging, lifting flesh, fat blood, the irons
as it's written!
that Thomas of Monmouth saw
they pin them up like Christ
               have them for mawkins

                        trussed like pigs
                        jabbed with thorns
and scalded all over with water, gorping!
no wonder that night a tempest blew in
yowing murder!
                        and all them lords will have no truck -
                        'was no crucifixion by his wounds'!
Pah! Ask you Thomas that!
a Jew covers his art,
makes it look like what it's not
                        hides dark doings with all his fashion
                        as dirt he sweeps to cover his cloven track
                        and by that you know his work!
and old Theobald, he heard some barney
over where to bury him!
a witness!
                        now that would be a caution
                        and none denied!
                        a martyr, our William
                        little lamb, a pure and bonny godson!
mark then, that is why they chose him
remember you those lights, fairy glowing
I saw with my own eyes
dancing pink about his body in the wood
                        and just late, a rose bush, thornless smooth
                        sprouting sudden on his grave!
sick mawthers healed!
                        and all his enemies fairing badly!
the serpent has raised him saintly!
                        and by St William
                        just as well
                        we send that devil back to hell!

Joseph Ben Solomon of Norwich

What is this city?
Its rampancy, I do not know it:
this rummaging of the ear,
this rankling in the skin,
this swelling, muttering increase.

Who is this?
I do not know them, up all night
polishing their desire,
they who see in its nacreous globe
themselves doubled, and are flattered by it.

What a fair outside falsehood has.

Thomas of Monmouth?
That credulous armpit!
Would see a horse in a handbasket
should it suit him,
and ride it too!

The convert Theobald?
A rat, *and* its arse!
And would strangle his own mother
to burrow an inch more
into the Christian heart!

How gladly you do let him
and compose your flinty faces
as though it did not hurt.
Liars!
Madness!

Are you men and women,
or are you wyrms?
The very ground seems riddled
and likely to fall head down

                into the red dark.

Hush, hush,
these are just a thin sliver
hissing its discontents.
No matter if it slither and snap,
Truth protects us, I put my faith in that.

Licoricia, daughter of Joseph Ben Solomon of Norwich

Who's this?
Pim pom skilly, kitten and pie.
Why, it's Moggy, when it's foggy,
purr purr pouncing, 2 green eyes.

Who's this?
Pim pom skilly, kitten and pie.
In the yard there's a doggy,
woof woof walking, 12 feet high.

The People

rake up your courage, you scanty lights
and burn
                be fat with firing
    keep at home if you be feared
                        of grass snakes
I've need of blood, not piss and milk,
                  nor ought your water
him who pulls his linens above his head,
leave not your bed   nor show your face
this night nor ever after
                stick we,
                    a nail in the bowels of history
slick as the harnser spearing
                go out the castle's shadow, cross the street

crush crush
my boots are thirsty
crack crack
    the garden rat is wise to run
        Who's there?   us
        Who's there?   let me in
        Who's there?   dowse the candles
flick spittle,
    liquorice black
for love
    it spitting loudly
seize a snake by his head,   bundle him
        for light to see
pinch out the littl'uns
    most of all,
        the barrel, scrape it
crack
worst to leave a filth to spread
for love
    stuff it in a sack
    and the cat,   no less a Jew
    are you purgers or are you pansies?
    godless yowling, gabble
for light for love
leave the corn stubble black
for love for light
    close the door
    the garden rat is wise to run
    go out the castle's shadow, cross the street

    go to the well
scrape scrape
my boots are thirsty
    go to the well
        for love
        pour out that foulness
for light
spitting loudly, yowling

                        down in the dark, hear them
                        shut like ledgers
                                        snap snap
tight then tighter pack
        blue then purple then black

they crawled from the pit,
        we only put them back

Well

            WOWOWOW
                    OWOWOW   WOW

dawn. routs. out.
toad. stone. folk.
grit. piss. wet. cloud.

                OWOWOW
                        WOWOW   AA

stone. stand. odd. all.
i. burst. cram. skin.
six. big. ten. small.

            AA   WOW OW
                                OW

and. one. crumped. head.
child. hole. howl.
on. stink. flesh. floor.

        OW OW
                    AA

week. of. flies.
thirst. wind. it.

dawn. die. noise

AA

turned. face. them.
crowd. O. mouths.
round. eyes. coins.

The Corpse of William Speaks

Where have I gone?
Blood in the milk
and a skilly pim pom

Ask the slow worm
swaddling my thumb

He gives hot cake
He gives cold tongue

O Ma n' Pa,
they'd like to know...

BANG, says the star!

Ha
      Ha
            Ha

Five Postcards from Norwich Castle

Stopping here and there, a tourist readies their camera

    I.   Battlement

Lookout!
Camera action! Clap!
A calamitous azure!
And periwinkle perhaps, or cyan!
The sagacity!
At any rate, Jacquard swathes of panoramas,
(in topaz, or chalcedony?) are
as shrapnel shards, over decades, that inch their way to the heart.

When the angel drops that penny, the sky,
I snap!

    II.   Dungeon

In the sub cellar below black,
death masks! shackles! sundry crooks
say: wet as leeches! small as moles!
say: how gloats the crowd, although
not *quite* as glib as stone!
say: cheese!
(The barbarity!)
If I see Martha's ghost, I'll shake the bitch's hand!
but no thank you to her billhook!

Wish you were here.

    III.   King Gurgunt Under the Mound

Gurgunt, Gurgunt!
Pose: enthroned, with sword in front!
A cramped coil that Gurgunt, poised to spring at direst moment!

Background: the Saxon hoard, skeletons, silver cups,
a big jewel, a golden *ring, ring...*
Gurgunt? Gurgunt, Hello?...

...

The audacity!
Gurgunt, Gurgunt,
Don't be a shit!
Hurry up.

      IV.   Natural History

Lemur! Lions! Polar bear! A rhino's head!
Great auk (and eggs)! Bustards! Butterflies!
Owls, Rat, Crocodile! O,
the humanity!

Companions, now we see you face to face!
by loosened tongue of artifice!
You gossiping darks, draped on dreaming's resonance!

Tiger, Tiger, who storms my forests of delight!
The kiln of your eye
has burned away impurity!

      V.   The Devil Dances on the Walls

Who saw Him? *Just us.*
(A double exposure!)

When? *When the arcading was not long done.*
(The depravity!)

How did you know Him? *By the stench.*
(Oh my!)

Which dance was He doing? *The mazurka.*
(But of course!)

What did He look like? *Like a live lung growing clumps of hair.*

It: Mazurka? Such lies. I never did any
such thing.

No wonder,
eye nor lens have never kenned
the pits I place my paw prints in.
Nor that air-thin silk, my shame, neither.

University of East Anglia

Under the light of the moon a lone rabbit passes through the graveyard of poets

Black human eyes, wet and rocking
in their nests of dry grass.
The white moon is not a symbol,
the moon is a coin they pass around
and around. So, their blue tongues and hands
grow tired of making to her their signs,
they recline into the earth, who spits them up again
as grass.
The blood is a red bead
where the tip is snapped and sucked,
where I creep and eat, eat the wet eyes
in the grass,
who follow me without mouths.
How very unlike those precise thorns,
the stars.

The ear says to the mouth,
the mouth listens to the ear:
better that no one will know you,
no one knows you even now.

Look at the enormous stone slabs like carefully risen chests,
and at the stone stairs like slit snakes,
at the high stone passages, obelisks, daisies
made of moonlight, where no one has ever existed,
though sometimes there goes beggared Thought
with a voice like delicate pages turning.

Too late you see how the lake becomes a silver mirror
and so do the trees, the flints, the darkness,
and the sneaking threads of secret streams.

What use to say of this thick-cut coldness

I love you, this coldness who crushes
my hot ingot heart like a nut.
I don't live on love,
I live on the shadows of enormous slabs,
black eyes and bloody grass,
grass that strokes such a rabbit,
strokes it like a copper toy, and says
if only you tried hard enough to stop this rabbiting.

And then, over it all,
came the white owl, Silent Death.

Strangers

A canary in a gilded cage begins to sing

Who him?

Who him from?

Is him him? Or is him not?

That not him nest him in?

That not him yellow egg? Him yellow butter?

If him not him, then who him is?

If him not cat, then is him dog?

Where him called?

Where him seeds scattering then?

If house dark? If mirror not glint?

If egg full of blood? If him blood lay egg?

So who him *then?*

Who belong him?

Is him strange?

Him him cage?

But where him *him?*

How long him take?

Is him cuckoo?

Him tooth bite out him tooth?

Him nail pluck out him eye?

Him left hand tie him right hand laces?

Why? Why him cut him noses?

For spite him faces?

Tunnels

A sunny day on a Norwich city street

come down   you   true root and   crawl into elbow's   crook low   under
odourless colourless frozen tons come   tip on those soft worms your toes lose those old
            closed doors   your hours along   the gnawed   moving
rope of mouth   come home only   know long corners   know who holds
you close no   longer loud   go alone   our scoured spool   loops of   sour
       follow hole   of broke tongue   come belong   who could not   want to know
what lopes along   our crack-drowned   howling the   softly   sound   of

          pounding hoof

Witches

Five strange figures meet on St Andrew's Hill at midnight.

1

nettle child, all hooked and eyed
and nestled in the crescent
come here and stitch your little middle
you bark, we bite
so if you screw it, do it tight

2

he who draws up the dark, saying *sunshine* -
in private, his eyes
to roll down his tongue, and stick
in public, his tongue
to slide from his eyes, and drip

3

cat by the rosemary
cat on the bed
cat brought gold and mouse skin gloves
wink and tell her
what you'd like instead

4

right hand red with dog meat
the moon slips on her diamond leash
and follows me
sighing, glancing
raining sequin seeds

5

hear that? *Its* teeth (icicles!)
click on air that's not our ankles!
we go up and down
come chunks of luck
that fence the world, a frozen flood!

In a nearby ally, where It *had been watching,* It *stands, then slowly* It *walks away.*
And, where It *had sat in the summer night,*
a patch of frost.

Will Kemp

I sense a crafty creeper at my ear,
Peeping from the close dark as if to hear
A story. Well, given your quiet art,
I'll reward that spidery ardour, and start.
        The greatest Fool in all this foolish world...
No? But you have two ears, so must have heard
Of Kemp! His fame is like a galleon's gliding keel
To whom all Triton's pearly horses kneel;
Quick he draws his throng, like tides, about him,
Then fleet and fast, dancing through, he parts them.
Like the hare, he counts a mile but a leap,
Out-bounds all coursing jaws, out-frisks their keep;
He winks his amber eye in honey rolled
And before him they toss a road of gold.
And his wit! Hinted, like the moon's shy blush
Behind a cloud, then lights with sudden flush
The stunned, immaculate, dumb-staring ground.
You'd think his voice must needs be booming loud,
No! As ice, which in silent Winter glistens,
When it cracks, each creature stops, and listens.
And since you know Kemp, you'll know his Wonder:
In nine scant days, through snow, slough and thunder,
He danced from London to Norwich! But few
Are they that know the tale and know it true.
        Hear now, on the wind, his speech! Clear as bells
That chime to coasts, fens, and eleven hells.
Let's follow it, over tree-top and roof,
Come quickly now, through chimney smoke we move
To Norwich and an Inn there. Quietly,
Press your eye against the glass. Can you see
That man there? Watch, as hand over his heart,
Our Kemp himself recounts the missing part.
        'Good Norwich sirs, fine and merry, I could
Not wish for better company, for good,
Kind ears to hear this, my strangest story –

Fantastic, brave, full of sound and fury!
Friends, scholars, it is three years to the eve
I, dancing, met this city's gate. I'm grieved
Now that I must own myself a liar.
O! Do not misunderstand me! Fire,
Wroth, and irons could not make gentle Kemp
A cheat! He danced every step, and rightly tamped
All slander, and rightly cashed his wager.'

    'I have, for fear, hidden what transpired there,
Fear that they may call Kemp mad, or some fair
Fancy-peddler, as crass as such are cheap.
But now, the time for truth is ripe to reap.
I beg, lend me the treasure of your time
And I'll pour out these dainty pearls of mine.'

    'That chill night, at St Giles Gate I stood,
The fading Lenten sky a streak of blood;
Bone-sore, perished, my merry almost gone,
Quietly I crept to respite. There upon
I sudden heard – what? – like leaves and laughter,
Like snowdrops jostling, with sighing after.
The tabor beat fainted and died away,
My friends melted; alone, I went astray.
Between tall trees that I could not recall,
I saw light, a dimpling, yolk-coloured ball
Like winter solstice sun, as dusk as dawn –
And moved by queer temptation, I was drawn.
Then, too late, I looked back at where I'd come:
But the road by which I'd entered was gone.
I thought: this place is Norwich no longer,
Or perhaps, some deeper Norwich, stronger,
Older, darker, longer. Yet on I pressed;
Kemp is not frail of heart, nor soon distressed,
he guessed that out lay further in, and so
he chased that light through blackness all aglow,
The misty air to rainbows darkening,
The living trees with starlight sparkling.'

    'Now, if you be feeble, then sit you down,
For there, frightening wonders skulked all around.

I saw dolls made of corn, who'd float consumed
by flames but would not burn, they lit the gloom
with pink and blue, making infants' mewling;
I saw wooden arms from branches reaching,
with mushroom nails, and gloves of lichen lace;
I saw a black cat with a woman's face
Pounce on mice who cried like little children,
And white china cows were weeping for them;
I saw mouths smiling among the flowers,
Sensed a presence that, unseen, devours
The future like a sucked, receding string;
By a still pool, I heard a mermaid sing,
And when she turned I saw her single eye,
A lamprey's mouth that flexed with no reply.
At that last, I paled and quickened my pace,
Then, I came to the stomach of that place.
In a ring of holly trees bent and low,
A dark so tight no light could come nor go,
I saw two enormous eyes, round and green
Like a dog's, flashing in the night, a sheen
Of horn, mane, and brawn, full wide as a bull,
But it stood like a man, and in my skull
I smelled the sweetly drunken scent of rose,
Heard the laboured breath as from the shadows
Stepped a most fine attired gentleman!'

    'The stranger stood no less than ten feet tall,
Was arrayed in emeralds and sand-sized pearls,
His silk doublet was teal and sea-foam blue
And silvered like night waves beneath the moon,
He had eyes like a mare's, as large as black,
His skin was nettle-green, he had the knack
Of smiling did this queer, handsome fellow.
Then, he doffed his owl-feather hat, and low
He bowed and said: 'Will Kemp! What a pleasure
That I entertain your kindly leisure!
Why, news of your fooling has travelled far,
I had hoped to meet you, and here you are!
Welcome Kemp, to Fairyland, whereupon

I am the King, Old Oberon.' Said I:
    'My dear King, it is the highest honour,
But alas, poor Kemp cannot stay longer;
Provided he pass through the city wall
Kemp shall be crowned The Greatest Fool of All,
So, with dues and sad regret I say
That I must go and dance my merry way.'
A sudden darkness drew across his brow,
Which creased, like a swell cut before the prow.
He said: 'Kemp, I believe you do not know
The dire despair of the path you go,
For, due to the dread magics here enmeshed,
The way's closed to those not of fairy flesh;
You may dance away, but you will wander
For a thousand years thither and yonder
In mazes, ever aging, unto dust."
    'Having heard this grim part, I trust
You must be puzzling how I stand here.
I am Kemp, always merry, never drear,
Not ever have I told a tragedy.
Curious? Then toss poor Kemp a penny
And you may hear his secrets. Sirs, ready?
Draw up your stools, raise your ale, and hear me.'
    'I went wan, shook from head to toe, distraught,
But not for long, on a sudden - I thought!
Said I: 'Kind King, there's much you've heard of me,
My dancing, jigging, my jokes most merry,
How sad t'would be to not complete my quest,
For Kemp to nevermore dance, jape and jest;
Sure, for the love you have of me, a chance -
I'll wager you, my freedom for a dance!
Allow me to out-jig your best, and if
I win, your magic parts, I leave and live.'
At that, I saw the Fey King sweetly smile
Like one who knows he also has his wiles.
'A fair bet, and if I may say, well put,'
He said, 'But, should I win, I'll take your foot.'
I paused, he was indeed sly this Fey King,

For how cruel to thieve from Kemp his dancing!
I agreed it, though stunned and all agog.
'Great Kemp,' he challenged, 'please, out-dance my dog.'
I laughed then, thinking myself quite clever.
'Your dog, of course. Where is the pup? Never
Have I had the pleasure to dance with one
Of such esteem. Pray, what's his name: Bon Bon,
Mince Pie, Woofsy, perhaps Lord Twinkle Paw?'
Then, it was as if the world had withdrawn,
Then, sweetest Sound shut her lips in despair,
Gentle Light gave up and died in the air,
All was frigid, empty, old like the grave,
When in *It* padded on an oily wave
Of misery. I felt that stench of breath.
It said, 'Know me. I dance the dance of Death."

  'Before I could stutter, the dance began -
It swirled, traipsed and turned, upright like a man,
Its heavy steps, like stones, pounded the floor,
The dark flashed white where *It* flourished *Its* claws.
I felt my life had slunk from me and gone,
But Kemp had made a bet, so he struck on!'

  'Good sirs, I did my best to match *Its* steps,
and all the little strength that I had left
I roused! I turned and traipsed, I stepped and swirled,
Into that blackest pas-de-deux I hurled
Myself! Until, at the grand conclusion
It gaped *Its* jaws, and in the confusion,
Enticed me in to end the deadly dance.
My friends, I went, beguiled by the trance!
Yes, men, I stepped upon *Its* slimy tongue,
I passed *Its* teeth, beheld *Its* throat and lungs,
There the rotten air was faintly calling:
Will Kemp, Will Kemp. I felt myself falling –
Then reason broke upon me with a clap!
I flung myself aside! The jaws dropped – snap!'

  'Haggard and harried, I rolled on the dirt,
I was shaken, filthy, yes, but unhurt.
But before I'd thanked Sweet Mother Mary,

The Fey's shadow was leaning over me.
He said, 'So, your admirers do not lie;
Fellow fey, his claims mustn't be denied,
Look at him, illustrious Kemp – the fool."
    "Well met,' said I. He raised his emerald arm,
And with it he braided some wolfish charm
That smoked and coiled about me where I lay,
Then with a puff, breathed my right foot away.
'Will Kemp,' he said 'It is not my intent to torment
Poor fools who lose their way here, I lament
As much as you your long doom to wander
And now to drag your stump. Try no further
Kemp, you suffer enough.' 'Wise King', said I,
'For your love of me, please, another try!
Yes, I am, as you rightly say, a fool,
But I so wish to be the foolest fool,
Even if now I must hop through that gate.
I can dance no more, yet I can still straight
Leap, as long as I have but one good leg.
Fey King, please, another wager, I beg,
Allow me to out-hop your best, and if
I win, your magic parts, I leave and live.'
Amused, the King discarded his glower,
Suddenly gentle, tame as a flower.
'Truly, you are a most singular man,'
Said Oberon, 'so, whatever your plan,
It would be my honour to see it through.'
Yet, in my soul it seemed a dread wind blew.
'A fair bet,' he said 'and again, well put,
But should I win, I'll take your other foot."
    'Fine gentlemen, I know what you're thinking -
How could Kemp face him twice without quailing?
How brave, how manfully he breached the heat
Of danger's flames – but why has he two feet?
Just pour him a cup of your finer ale,
And he'll gladly tell the remaining tale.'
    'Said he, 'Kemp, get up from that muddy knoll,
And kindly,' he challenged, 'out-jump my doll.'

This time, I held my tongue and followed him;
He swept us up in a summery skim
Of air and we twinkled over the dusk,
Landing with a skirl of shimmering dust
In some darkling marsh, grim and desolate,
The only crying a lonely cricket.
We stood hard by a little ditch, and there
A silent corn dolly floated and flared.
'For sure,' I laughed, 'this cannot be your trick!
Even your dolly here could jump this ditch.
Why, look at her legs, those powerful nubs,
See her waggling arms, like fine chubby grubs,
And the chasm, it is so very large,
It seems a thousand feet from marge to marge.
Scarce can Kemp compete! Oh, what shall he do?
But I jest; for this mercy, I thank you."
   'At that, the small dolly took to the air,
So I braced myself, bent low and prepared
My finest spring. Kemp launched, he sailed, he flew!
He would land like a cat, as soft as dew!
But something, I felt, was terribly wrong,
That momentary leap grew very long,
And longer and longer; the other bank
Dwindled away, and it seemed I had shrunk
To a flea, cast out on an inky void;
I forgot my name, a strange current toyed
With me, I, like a bottle on the sea
Was a lost nothing, bobbing and empty;
I fell then, I fell down and down and down,
And at the bottom, I fell again – down.
Stay with me, the deep said, lullaby-light,
And just as I sunk me down to sleep, fright
Seized me! Then, I thrashed like a speared fish,
I kicked, screeched, and swam, and woke in the ditch.
I was soaked, cold, and dangling by one arm
From the farther bank, blanched, yes, but unharmed.
But before I could breathe the mortal air,
Noiseless, the Great Fey was lingering there.

'A fool twice over is fool to the core,'
He said, 'the world needs not a single more."
      "Well met, again,' said I. Again, the smoke
Fell down dark about me, and when it broke
On a breath, both my precious feet were gone.
He spoke softly then, did King Oberon:
'Poor Kemp, never to dance another dance,
No jig to jump, and no Morris to prance,
What is he then if he cannot fool? Sad.
Will Kemp, truly I am fond of you, had
There been a way, know I would have sent you,
For those who dare to wager me are few.
I'm not cruel; it pains me to see you thus –
Try no further Kemp, you suffer enough."
      'I pondered long upon my sorry state,
But could not lie beneath the tread of fate,
Kemp had laid his path and he would finish,
He'd stand and blaze, not dim and diminish.
'Fair King,' said I 'for true, you do speak fair,
Of two-time fools the wide world has its share,
But three-time fools are very rare. Do not
Deprive it of its best; King, a last shot,
A final toss for Kemp to prove his worth,
Please, let him be the greatest fool on Earth.
I have no feet, all dancing I have quit,
Ay, jumping too, but this fool has his wit –
I'll wager you a mental duel, and if
I win, your magic parts, I leave and live.'
Whether this mighty King then smiled or frowned
I could not say, but he made a sad sound.
'A fair bet,' he sighed 'and indeed, well said,
But should I win, this time I'll take your head."
      'Gentlemen, these were words of heavy dread,
Well you know that for Kemp to lose his head
Were death. I knew it too, and acquiesced.
But dear friends, please, do not be so distressed,
Kemp's tale is not yet done, though it be grim,
Pray, be silent now, and listen to him.'

'Once more up-curled that cloud of shining sand,
Once more we soared on vernal air to land
Once more within that ring of holly trees,
Where our dazzling trail still played in the breeze.
An intensity squatted in that den,
Iron-dense, it pressed hard and low, as when
Voiceless lightening whips the sky asunder,
And cowering beasts await the thunder.
It was not until then I thought the King
Peculiar: his huge eyes like shining,
Cold, polished coals, which never blinked nor strayed,
His skin that was smooth as glass, green as jade,
He towered like an oak before it falls,
and when he grinned, the shadows cringed, appalled.
'Kemp, I respect you too much for mercy,'
Said he, 'Now, your challenger shall be me;
Answer me a riddle to show your wit,
And you shall leave this cursed place with it.'
'A noble wager,' I said, 'good brother,
I vow on it, one man to another."
Then, smiling, he leaned in close and whispered
In my ear. This, my friends, is what I heard:
'Everyone is me, but no *one* is me,
they all know how to call me, easily,
and call whether or not they know my name,
They are never not speaking to me, shame,
For when they speak I greet them. Who am I?'
Long I thought, for well I knew the danger,
But, to these such guiles, Kemp was no stranger.
Said I, 'All yet none? Then this is a crowd.
Unnamed, yet called? Always answers, unproud?
Then this must be a pleasant mob for once.
Dear King, the answer is: *an audience.*'
At that, it seemed that every atom sighed;
If trees and rocks weren't dumb, they would have cried.
'O Kemp, I so had hoped you'd give it true,
What a pity, the right answer is *you.*"
'The great beast Despair beset me at last

And even Kemp began to weep, aghast
At the strength of its terrible paw. 'O!'
I cried, 'O! –
> A single drop of gall has soured all the milk of kindness,
> And this once fair World can be nothing now
> but that curd beneath my crawling knees.
> What is the rose without my brushing by?
> It appalls me. What is the moon,
> If she should go on shining, and me gone?
> A festering sore. All I have loved is a cold rebuff
> And, harlot, I curse its persistence.
> But who is this madman I hear raving?
> Not I, surely, not I who have loved this life
> Even unto my undoing.
> For love of you, sweet World,
> For all your leaping delights
> I have doomed myself;
> In my haste to return,
> O well-spring of all my joy,
> I die. O weariness.
> Forgive that hasty tongue,
> I know not myself in this grief
> Of losing you.
> Life, my love, forget me.'

'I kneeled and awaited my sentencing
When I saw a change come upon the king.
He said, 'I truss you in a chain of debt
Kemp, but our story needn't finish yet;
How charmingly you have spoken, how fair,
A fool you may be, but your heart is there,
Sober as any stone on the cold earth.
Tell me Kemp, do you truly sue for mirth,
Of all fools, must you be the greatest?
Speak carefully now,' he said, 'do not jest'.
I beseeched, 'Dear King, more than anything!
And anything I would do!' Said the king:
'I have won, I shall have your feet and head,
But I may lend you fairy flesh instead,

With those, you may merrily walk away,
But hark, dark is the day one deals with fey.'
Said I, 'Dark are all the long days of death,
And to be forgotten, a darker death
Even than that, so I accept your lease,
Grant me these fey limbs, great Oberon, please."

  'At that, the hexing smoke up-surged and swirled
and covered me whole. For a flash the world
vanished, it was so quick I thought I dreamed,
and yet, how long and full of noise it seemed.
But when it cleared, my God! I had two feet!
Stronger, fleeter and sparkling with a sweet
Fairy light, and all my sight, my new eyes
Flashing with rainbow fire! To my surprise,
My wits were somehow keener, miracle
Indeed! But the Fey smiled like a jackal
In the haze. 'Now Will Kemp,' he said 'be gone!"

  'He clapped his immense hands and thereupon
I was snatched from the spot, yanked on a string
It seemed, howling backwards, flying, speeding,
While before me, strange scenes payed out like rope;
I saw, as it came whipping into scope,
That monstrous forest by which I had come,
Dark, green, and dense teeming with frightful scum;
No sooner was it plucked away again,
And I bowled through a cathedral heaven
Of rosy gems, who did glow and smother,
City-large, and chime to one another;
In turn, they snapped away, then all around
Me howled a sapient wind, and no ground,
No sky, only desolate fingering
Of angry gusts, and their long lingering
In the sad, sly, eternal dusk - then bang!
I crashed upon my back. I could have sang!
For when I looked up, I saw all my friends,
Stunned! Yes, my adventure was at its end,
For there, to my amaze, was St Giles Gate,
And the sky still showed only evening late.'

      'O, you merry souls, well you know the rest:
Good Will Kemp danced into Norwich, he pressed
Through crowds as glad as thick, admirers all!
And when the surge bore him to St John's wall
He leapt it, strong as a stag, as a hare!
Stronger than any there – or anywhere.
I may have winked then, but I held my tongue
In fear of that green devil, Oberon.
And so you know this be no tale, no chase,
Get you to the guild hall and see the place
Where your mayor himself nailed up my shoes
To show you all: what Kemp bets, Kemp then proves!'
      Well, well. Now my crafty creeper, you know
Kemp's tale. Tell me, did you enjoy his show?
My, how the wily hero kept them rapt,
How they whistled, how stamped their feet and clapped!
But now, to each his own haunt goes slinking,
And leaves Kemp by a lone candle, drinking.
What a shame that his crowd has thinned and gone,
But lucky for you, the tale isn't done.
Ah! He bids goodnight to this dreary inn,
Come, let us prowl behind and follow him.
      Hush now, worried is the gossiping brush,
And fleet of foot is the chattering rush
Of wind on which we sail, and cold and dark
Is the small heart that stops and feels its mark -
On the road, a frightened man is turning,
Alone, he thought, yet his ears are burning.
'Who's there? Who's there, I say! I cannot see!'
      'Will Kemp,
It's three years the eve you borrowed from me,
Three years since you begged I make you a fool
Three years I watched, waited, calmly and cool;
It's true I am not a mortal man,
I honour my promises, here I am;
I know you know there is something I lack,
Those fairy feet, that head, I want them back.'
'No, by Mary! Devil, you cannot be!'

'Poor old Kemp, who vanished from history,
Grave unmarked, not a soul knew he was dead,
For there was just some fool who'd lost his head'.

It: And now the Sea is touching my salt-stung foot;
that sly, slinking Sea,
ever-chattering mouth Sea,
lifting like a bone from the flesh Sea.

My shadow, are you?
Eater, thinly, and without discretion,
a black line drawn across much too far.

Come then, dog that you are.
It's time.

Flint

Norwich meets its end.

The sun disguises himself as a smoldering coal,
the moon has turned away her face, and gone.
How did it become so late?
How is it that the sky is now a sheet of iron?
How could it be rusted and dropping its crumbs?

>My wormlings are gone,
>my pebbles, all the little hoodlums. Where?

Look, the once-far Sea knocks on my door,
the once-far Sea leans like a mountain,
the Sea is a boiling line drawn up against my chilly skin. Since when?
The soil is syrup, the light is blood, the foul air full of foam.
It is late; I have been made to be alone.

>No, *not alone.*
>In the near-to I see *It,* and behind *It, It* drags the flood.

You, You stretch of gut,
slow crawling with dog's hunger,
You, and the red nail-hole of *Your* eye,
and *Your* oozing thunder, how dare *You?*
You godless grub, grot-skulk, grave-gannet!

Are we all gizzards for *Your* gullet?
Are *You* nothing but stalk, beleaguering, haranguing?
Black mold, answer us!
Don't *You* turn away,
don't leave us!

That sound, like brass and tearing,
that tremble-gaping in the ground;
my gravel shivers, the grass is afraid.

Bulks are rising, rot spouts, a bubbling froth of bone;
up come my plague pits, my potter's fields, my fifty churchyards -

    the earth is giving up her dead

my dead.
Their star-bright skulls, I know them all by name,
and the numbers of those pearls, their teeth.
Where are you all off to, shining like that?
Why do you walk in a line? My loves, don't go –

but mud-spat, glowing, they follow *It*,
little candles, creatures made of sticks,
and one by one are doused in the Sea, with a hiss:
in the hand-that-made-them Sea,
in the judgement Sea, in the end-of-the-endings Sea.

      Must *You* leave nothing?
      Not even their bones to comfort me?

How dark it is now, as dark as *You*.
In the dark I can feel it, the sheet of the tide
is sliding over me, pulled by a hot hand;

I hear Wensum's lullaby die away,
I hear the cathedral bell softly knocking
beneath a wave, once, twice, three;

the fen has filled with quiet sand.

Where have the stars gone? Where is the wind?
There is only water's cold tongue,
water's fingers in my pockets.

There is salt and sad caresses,
there is a silent mile above my head.
Where is this? I do not recall this death.

I do not recall.

Who's there?

It: All shall be well,
all shall be well,
and all manner of things
shall be made well.